# The Feelings Book
## Journal

by Dr. Lynda Madison
illustrated by Josée Masse

★ American Girl®

This journal
belongs to

...................................................

...................................................

Published by American Girl Publishing

16 17 18 19 20 LEO 12 11 10 9 8

Editorial Development: Therese Maring, Michelle Watkins, Carrie Anton
Art Direction and Design: Chris Lorette David, Camela DeCaire
Production: Tami Kepler, Judith Lary, Paula Moon, Kristi Tabrizi

Illustrations: Josée Masse

**Dear Reader,**

As you grow up, it's only natural to have many different feelings. These days, you may notice that your feelings change quickly or even that you seem to be juggling several different feelings at once! You may be happy one minute, then down in the dumps, and then go back to feeling happy again.

Strong feelings can make it seem as if you're spinning out of control. But all your feelings—good and bad—can guide you in making smart decisions in your life. Listening to your heart and understanding your emotions can help you be true to yourself and sort out the tricky and sticky situations you face every day.

This companion journal to *The Feelings Book* is filled with checklists, quizzes, and strategies for learning more about your feelings. Fill in the pages. Jot down your thoughts. Take a quiz and answer a few questions. But most of all, think. Have fun learning about yourself, and celebrate the special person you are!

**Your friends at American Girl**

# All About You

**You are the only one of you there is.**
That makes you a V.I.P.—a Very Important
Person! You have special likes, dislikes,
hobbies, and activities that make you
different from other people. **Take time
to remember what makes you unique.**

# Some Facts About Me

My name is _____

Sometimes people call me by my nickname, _____

_____

I'm in _____ grade in school.

I live with _____

_____

_____

_____

_____

I enjoy _____

_____

_____

_____

_____

_____

I am good at _____

_____

_____

_____

_____

At school, I like to _____

_____

_____

_____

_____

On weekends, I like to _____

_____

_____

_____

_____

# My Friends

One way to look at your connections with others is by making a Friend-o-Gram. Put your name in the middle square and your friends' names in the circles. Add as many circles as you want. Then, draw lines between the names of people who are also friends with each other.

Your Friend-o-Gram is a "snapshot" of the people you feel closest to. It can help you think about how you spend your time. Are there friends you haven't connected with in a while? Give them a call!

(Circle) the words that describe your friends.

## My very best friends are

honest    understanding    happy

helpful    smart    kind    supportive

funny    generous    talented

Fill in a name and check all the boxes that apply.

One friend I can really talk to is _____

She's good to talk to because she

☐ cares about me no matter what.

☐ listens without interrupting.

☐ doesn't influence me to do things her way.

☐ understands how I feel.

☐ asks what I think.

☐ has good ideas.

☐ checks with me later to see how things are going.

☐ can keep a secret, but would tell an adult if it was really important.

Some adults I can talk to are

_____ and _____

# My Favorite Things

Turn to, or think about, your favorite things when you need to feel comfortable and calm—or when you want to have fun!

Here are some of my all-time favorites:

Holiday _____

Place to travel _____

Color _____

Hobby _____

Clothes _____

TV show _____

Subject in school _____

Actor/Actress _____

Song _____

Movie _____

Stuffed animal _____

Real animal _____

Free-time activity _____

In my house, the room I feel the most comfortable in is

_____

Here's a sketch of this room:

Some ways I like to relax:

- [ ] Taking a bubble bath
- [ ] Sitting in a favorite cozy chair
- [ ] Getting a back rub
- [ ] Having my hair brushed
- [ ] Reading a book
- [ ] Writing

- [ ] Playing music
- [ ] Singing
- [ ] Taking a walk
- [ ] Talking with a friend
- [ ] Other _____
  _____
  _____

# Fun Time

Having fun with friends is a great way to relax, have a few laughs, and feel closer.

Here are ten things I like to do with my friends:

1. _____

2. _____

3. _____

4. _____

5. _____

6. _____

7. _____

8. _____

9. _____

10. _____

Long, private talks and quiet conversations with friends are important. (Circle) some of the topics you and your friends talk about.

school

parents

clothes

friends

feelings

sports

movies

boys

upcoming events

books

other_____

other_____

# Sleep Time

When you're rested, your mind is sharper than when you're tired. You can concentrate better and you're less likely to feel grumpy. When you miss out on ZZZs, even little troubles can seem worse than they are. How well do you sleep at night?

Most of the time, I

☐ sleep soundly all night.

☐ can't get to sleep.

☐ wake up in the night.

☐ have to drag myself out of bed in the morning.

☐ feel sleepy or tired all day long.

Most girls your age need at least ten hours of sleep every night to feel their best. Keep track for a few nights. Are you getting enough sleep?

|  | Bedtime | Waking Time | Number of Hours I Slept |
|---|---|---|---|
| Monday |  |  |  |
| Tuesday |  |  |  |
| Wednesday |  |  |  |
| Thursday |  |  |  |
| Friday |  |  |  |
| Saturday |  |  |  |
| Sunday |  |  |  |

What sometimes keeps me awake is _____

_____

_____

Sometimes, instead of going to bed on time, I _____

_____

_____

I might get more shut-eye if _____

_____

_____

# What's Your Reaction?

For each situation, pick the reaction that is closest to the way you would probably respond.

**1.** I thought my mom could take my friends and me to a movie, but it turns out she has to take my brother to track practice. My reaction is to

   **a.** stomp my foot, cry, and make sure my mother knows I don't appreciate this.

   **b.** rattle off all the reasons I want to go to the movie, then call my friends to complain.

   **c.** say it's OK and slink off to my room. There will always be another time.

**2.** I make the cheerleading squad after three years of hard work! I respond by

   **a.** turning a handspring right there in the hall. After all, I'm a cheerleader!

   **b.** telling everyone just how excited I am—even those people who already know.

   **c.** just smiling. I don't want to call attention to myself right now.

**3.** I told everyone I'd bring the snacks to the club meeting, but then I leave them at home! My reaction is to

   **a.** throw my hands in the air and scream, making sure everyone knows what a tragedy this is.

   **b.** explain to every person I see why I forgot.

   **c.** quietly promise to bring something special the next time.

**4.** The big school play is tomorrow and I'm suddenly nervous. I respond by

   **a.** snapping at people, saying "Leave me alone so I can practice!"

   **b.** calling all my friends and relatives to rehearse my part.

   **c.** sitting in my room, going over my lines again and again.

# Answers

## ☐ The Nuclear Reactor

If you had mostly **a** answers, your feelings are out there where everyone can see them. It's great that you don't hold things in—people are sure to know where you're coming from! Just take care not to react so quickly that you shut down communication with another person. If you immediately act angry when, underneath it all, you are actually sad, hurt, or scared, other people will get the wrong impression about how you feel. Pay attention to how your behavior affects others. You might not realize that you say or do things that hurt the people around you.

## ☐ The Talker

If you had mostly **b** answers, you let your feelings out by being chatty. Good—talking to others can help you sort through what you are feeling. But be careful to think before you speak, or you could say things you'll regret later. Take time to think about whether you are talking to people who actually want to hear what you have to say, and make sure your words are not hurtful in some way. And don't let your chattiness keep you from figuring out how you really feel.

## ☐ The Private "I"

If you had mostly **c** answers, you may be great at solving problems by yourself, on your own schedule. Or you might be a very quiet or private person who does not want to burden others with your feelings. That can be fine, as long as you don't have a storm of emotions going on inside. If you do, you'll want to get your feelings out where you can take a good look at them, so they don't build up to the point that they make you ill. You might want to talk to others about how you feel so that they can offer help if you need it. Remember, talking to people can help them know that your quietness doesn't mean you're unfriendly.

# My Moods

Color in these mood thermometers to show how you've been feeling recently in each of these settings.

# At home:

## Happiness Thermometer

I'm sky-high happy!

Life is good!

I'm just so-so.

I'm down in the dumps.

## Anxiety Thermometer

I'm so tense, I can't move.

I worry a lot.

I barely feel nervous.

I'm as calm as can be.

## Anger Thermometer

I'm a one-girl explosion.

I'm starting to boil.

I'm holding things in so that I don't say things I shouldn't.

Everything's A-OK.

## Silliness Thermometer

I get giggling about lots of things.

I usually find something to laugh about.

I find it hard to take a joke.

Nothing really seems funny.

## At school:

### Happiness Thermometer

I'm sky-high happy!

Life is good!

I'm just so-so.

I'm down in the dumps.

### Anxiety Thermometer

I'm so tense, I can't move.

I worry a lot.

I barely feel nervous.

I'm as calm as can be.

### Anger Thermometer

I'm a one-girl explosion.

I'm starting to boil.

I'm holding things in so that I don't say things I shouldn't.

Everything's A-OK.

### Silliness Thermometer

I get giggling about lots of things.

I usually find something to laugh about.

I find it hard to take a joke.

Nothing really seems funny.

## When I'm with my friends:

### Happiness Thermometer

I'm sky-high happy!

Life is good!

I'm just so-so.

I'm down in the dumps.

### Anxiety Thermometer

I'm so tense, I can't move.

I worry a lot.

I barely feel nervous.

I'm as calm as can be.

### Anger Thermometer

I'm a one-girl explosion.

I'm starting to boil.

I'm holding things in so that I don't say things I shouldn't.

Everything's A-OK.

### Silliness Thermometer

I get giggling about lots of things.

I usually find something to laugh about.

I find it hard to take a joke.

Nothing really seems funny.

Your mood thermometer can help you take stock of how you're feeling about different parts of your life. Keep reading to learn more about your emotions and what you can do about them.

# Dealing with Your Feelings

You can learn about yourself by thinking back to times in your life when your feelings were very strong. For each of the emotions on the following pages, try to recall a situation in which you felt that way, what you thought, what you did, and what happened next.

The **Mood Minder** pages help you figure out the best way to deal with the ups and downs of each feeling.

# Feeling Happy

Whether you're on top of the world or just satisfied with life, you're probably happy much of the time. If you think about the times you've felt happy—what you were thinking and the things that you did—you may be able to bring back that happy feeling when down.

A time I felt very happy was when _____

_____

_____

_____

I felt happy because _____

_____

_____

When I felt happy, thoughts like this went through my mind:

_____

_____

_____

At the same time, I also felt

☐ hopeful.          ☐ inspired.          ☐ safe.

☐ optimistic.       ☐ capable.           ☐ silly.

☐ excited.          ☐ strong.            ☐ anxious.

☐ awed.             ☐ competent.         ☐ other _____

☐ joyful.           ☐ creative.          _____

☐ proud.            ☐ trusting.          _____

My body reacted to my happiness. I felt this emotion most in my

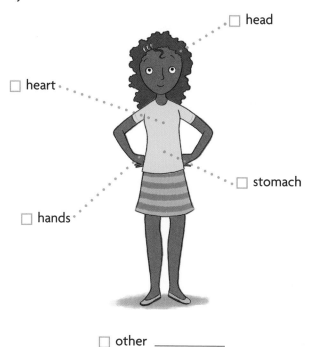

☐ head

☐ heart

☐ stomach

☐ hands

☐ other _____

# Mood Minder: I'm Happy

It's important to do things to commemorate your happiest times. Don't miss a chance to pass your happiness on to others, either!

I remember my happy times by

☐ looking at photos.

☐ taking photos.

☐ thinking back through memories.

☐ keeping awards and certificates.

☐ making a scrapbook.

☐ talking about my memories.

☐ writing in my journal.

☐ keeping souvenirs, such as

_____

_____

☐ other _____

_____

_____

Doing nice things for others can help them feel happy.
Surprise! That can make you feel happy, too.

I have done these things for someone else:

☐ Held a door open

☐ Given a gift

☐ Said something nice, such as _____

☐ Had lunch with someone

☐ Read a book to someone

☐ Cleaned

☐ Carried something

☐ Babysat

☐ Volunteered to _____

☐ Sat with someone new at school

☐ Did this special thing: _____

This week, I could make _____ happy by

_____

_____

_____

_____

# Feeling Scared

Sometimes it's fun to be scared—like when you're on a roller coaster. When you encounter something genuinely dangerous, such as a mean dog or a speeding car, your body's reaction to feeling scared can actually help you think fast and stay safe.

Other times you may feel frightened about things that aren't really dangerous at all, which isn't fun or helpful! Or you may stay afraid a long time after something has scared you. Learning how you reacted when you were scared in the past may help you be braver the next time around.

I felt scared when _____

_____

_____

_____

I was afraid because I thought something bad would

happen, like _____

_____

_____

My body reacted to my feelings of fear. I felt this emotion most in my

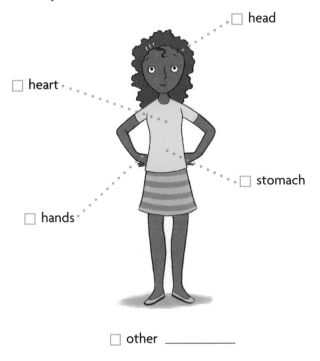

☐ head

☐ heart

☐ stomach

☐ hands

☐ other _____

I reacted to my fear by _____

_____

What helped me feel better was _____

_____

Some other things that scare me are _____

_____

# Mood Minder: I'm Scared

When you're scared, the best thing you can do is to calm yourself down so that you can think clearly. Deep, regular breathing allows your body to relax. One way to do this is to count slowly as you breathe deeply. Counting and breathing this way several times will help you control your fear.

When I do deep breathing, I will count to the number ____

A trustworthy friend can also help you calm down. Look for someone who understands why you're afraid but who isn't as scared as you are.

Someone I could talk to is

_____ or _____

Another strategy is to think of something pleasant to take your mind off things. Close your eyes and get a really clear picture in your mind of a comfortable place where you felt safe. Was it the beach, your favorite chair, a cabin in the woods, or someplace else?

A place I felt calm was _____

_____

Here's how this place looked: _____

_____

Sounds I heard when I was there: _____

_____

Scents I smelled there: _____

_____

Exercising your muscles can also help you relax. Put a check-mark next to the activities that work for you.

I can get active by

☐ walking.

☐ jogging.

☐ playing a sport, such as _____

☐ dancing.

☐ swimming.

☐ other _____

_____

# Feeling Anxious

Everyone worries now and then. Anxiety can hit you before a big test or performance, or when you think that bad things might happen. Sometimes you may feel uneasy for no particular reason at all. Can you think of a time when you felt anxious? Fill in the blanks and check the boxes below.

I felt anxious when _____

_____

_____

My body reacted to my anxiety. I felt this emotion most in my

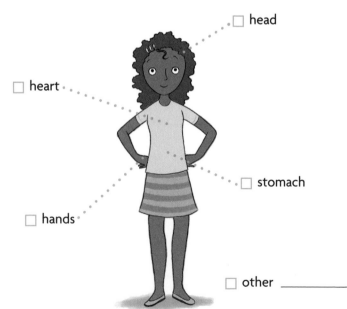

☐ head

☐ heart

☐ stomach

☐ hands

☐ other _____

I worried something bad would happen like _____

_____

_____

_____

I reacted to this feeling by _____

_____

_____

_____

My actions made things

☐ better          ☐ the same          ☐ worse

Other things that make me anxious are _____

_____

_____

_____

_____

# Are You a Big Worrier?

Are you as cool as a cucumber or more of a worrywart? Pick the answer that is closest to the way you would respond.

**1.** I'm doing pretty well in a class until—BOOM!—I get a bad grade on a quiz. I react by

   **a.** realizing that one bad score isn't the end of the world. I'll figure out how to study differently the next time.

   **b.** worrying about whether I'm smart, and thinking I'm sure to fail.

**2.** My teacher gives me a big part in the school play. I find myself

   **a.** excited about my new adventure, even when the going gets tough. This is fun!

   **b.** thinking of everything that could go wrong along the way, from forgetting my lines to tripping on my final bow.

**3.** When the seat of my pants rips in math class and everyone sees, I

   **a.** figure this could happen to anyone and realize that my classmates will stop joking soon.

   **b.** just know my life will be awful from here on out. I'll never live this down.

**4.** I wake up in the night and hear the wind whistling through my window. I decide to

- **a.** close my eyes and think pleasant thoughts until I fall back to sleep.
- **b.** lie there wide-eyed, imagining things much scarier than the wind that could be making that eerie howl.

# Answers

If you had mostly **a** answers, you tend to look on the bright side of things and feel confident in most situations. Share your positive outlook with others!

If you had mostly **b** answers, you tend to see mountains where there are only little bumps in the road. Worrying can make things worse than they are. Read on for some strategies to help you regain a positive focus.

# Mood Minder: I'm Anxious

Self-confidence is one of the best tools for fighting nervousness. You can learn to boost your confidence. Think about a time you kept your worries in check.

One time that I took charge of my worries was when _____

_____

_____

I told myself these positive things: _____

_____

_____

The next time you're worried, see if these thoughts calm you down:

Things will be OK in the end, because

☐ they always have been before.

☐ I have practiced or studied.

☐ I have confidence in myself.

☐ nothing really bad is likely to happen.

☐ I will still be a good person, even if I'm not the best.

☐ my friends will like me no matter what.

☐ other reasons _____

_____

_____

Distracting yourself from your negative thoughts can take your mind off your worries.

One activity I can do to distract myself is _____

_____

Something pleasant I can think about is _____

_____

A friend might tell me, "You don't need to worry because

_____

_____."

Having too much to do can add to your stress, which can make you more anxious. See if you can lighten your daily load of activities.

If I needed to, I could talk to my parents about cutting the following out of my schedule so that I wouldn't be as busy:

_____

_____

_____

_____

# Feeling Jealous

People call jealousy a green-eyed monster. We've all met that creature. The monster makes you think you aren't good enough the way you are, but he's wrong. Take charge! Celebrate your life and banish that jealousy monster forever.

I felt jealous when _____

_____

_____

_____

_____

_____

It made me think that _____

_____

_____

_____

_____

_____

My body reacted to my jealousy. I felt this emotion most in my

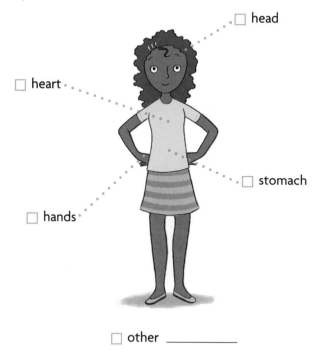

☐ head

☐ heart

☐ stomach

☐ hands

☐ other _____

I reacted by _____

_____

_____

Here's how the situation turned out: _____

_____

_____

# Mood Minder: I'm Jealous

To keep from getting jealous, focus on the good things in your life.

I am thankful for people like _____

_____

_____

I am thankful that I'm good at _____

_____

_____

_____

_____

Other things I like about myself and my life are _____

_____

_____

Jealousy can make you do and say things you feel bad about later on. Battle the urge to lash out when you're feeling jealous.

When I feel jealous, I will try not to

☐ make fun of anyone.     ☐ yell.

☐ take away someone's happiness.

☐ cry.

☐ get angry.

☐ do hurtful things.

Making goals can keep you focused on the future instead of on what you think your life is missing right now.

One goal that I have is to _____

Here are two things I can do to help me reach my goal:

1. _____

_____

2. _____

_____

# Feeling Disrespected

Sometimes people say or do things to you that
just aren't nice. Write about a time when you felt
picked on, bullied, or hurt.

I felt really disrespected when _____

_____

_____

_____

_____

My body reacted to my feelings. I felt this emotion most in my

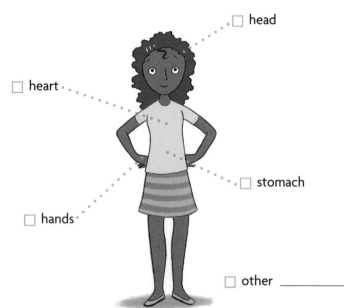

☐ head

☐ heart

☐ stomach

☐ hands

☐ other _____

I reacted to this feeling by _____

_____

_____

_____

_____

Here's how the situation turned out: _____

_____

_____

_____

_____

# Deal with Disrespect

If there's someone who regularly makes you feel bad, you shouldn't spend time with her, unless it's to try to improve your relationship. Talking to someone who disrespects you can be scary. A good first step is to write a practice letter that you don't plan to mail or even show to the person. The act of writing it can help you sort out your feelings and help you know what to say when you talk to this person again.

Dear _____ ,

The other day you _____

_____

_____

When that happened, I felt _____

_____

_____

I didn't like feeling that way. I don't know if you meant to do what you did, but would you please not do it again? Thank you very much.

Signed,

_____

When you do talk to the person who's making you feel bad, she may bring up something *you* did that made *her* feel angry or hurt. You may not have meant to hurt her at all. Write another practice letter to sort through how you might respond to her.

Dear _____ ,

I am sorry that I _____

_____

_____

_____

Next time, I'll try to _____

_____

_____

_____

Thanks for letting me know how you felt.

Signed,

_____

# Mood Minder: I've Been Dissed!

Don't get down when other people are mean to you. Think about how to respond. First, try to figure out if the person *meant* to be hurtful. Could you be oversensitive about what happened? Check the boxes that could apply.

This person might just have been

☐ busy.

☐ not aware.

☐ in a hurry.

☐ forgetful.

☐ worried about something else.

☐ trying not to look foolish.

☐ simply not thinking about my feelings.

No matter what happened, you are still a good person.
Remind yourself why.

Some things that I like about myself are _____

_____

_____

_____

Some adults I could ask to help me with this situation are

_____

_____

These people love and appreciate me: _____

_____

_____

_____

_____

# Feeling Angry

Everyone feels angry at times. You may be mad at another person, at a situation, or even at yourself. When was the last time you felt angry?

I felt really angry when _____

_____

_____

_____

_____

_____

People could tell I was angry because I _____

_____

_____

_____

_____

_____

Here's how the situation turned out: _____

_____

_____

_____

_____

_____

My body reacted to my anger. I felt this emotion most in my

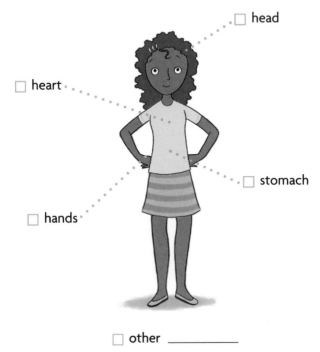

☐ head

☐ heart

☐ stomach

☐ hands

☐ other _____

When you're mad, other feelings can get mixed up with your anger. By recognizing those feelings, you can talk about them, too.

Some feelings I have when I'm angry are

☐ frustration.

☐ confusion.

☐ sadness.

☐ excitement.

☐ jealousy.

☐ anxiety.

☐ embarrassment.

☐ fear.

☐ hurt.

☐ other _____

Are you angry with someone? Writing a practice letter to that person can help you sort out your feelings. The letter isn't meant to be mailed. But writing truthfully about your feelings may help you discover what to do or say to help your situation.

Dear _____ ,

I feel angry right now because _____

_____

When you did that, I felt _____

_____

Maybe you didn't understand how I would feel. Next

time, would you please _____

_____

I'll do my part to make this situation better, too.

I will _____

Thank you.
Sincerely,

_____

# Mood Minder: I'm Angry

Lashing out at others can hurt your relationships. It can even get you into trouble. The first thing to do when you feel angry is to keep cool. Take a quick break so that you think before you act. Which "think break" could you take the next time you're angry?

☐ Breathe deeply for a minute.

☐ Count to ten before I take any action.

☐ Walk away for a minute, saying, "I need to think about what just happened."

☐ Find someone to talk to in private about the situation.

You can let your anger out without hurting people or things. Pick one of these safe ways to let off steam, so you don't say or do something you'll regret later.

☐ Punch a pillow            ☐ Dance

☐ Squeeze a ball            ☐ Other _____

☐ Take a walk or a run           _____

☐ Stomp on some                   _____
   bubble wrap                     _____

After you've calmed down, try talking directly to the person with whom you've been upset. Use this checklist to practice what you need to say.

When I'm angry with someone, I need to

☐ ask to talk for a few minutes.

☐ tell the person I didn't like how things went.

☐ ask if the person realized how I felt.

☐ ask to be treated differently next time.

☐ other _____

_____

_____

_____

_____

_____

# Feeling Lonely

Loneliness can happen when you wish you were with someone who's not around. You don't even have to be alone to be lonely. You may feel lonely when you think people around you don't understand or care about you. It can happen even when you are in a big crowd of people. Think about a time when you came down with a wicked case of the lonelies.

I felt lonely when _____

_____

_____

_____

_____

When I was lonely, I wished that _____

_____

_____

_____

_____

_____

This person might have understood how lonely I felt:

_____

Here's how the situation turned out: _____

_____

_____

_____

My body reacted to my loneliness. I felt this emotion most in my

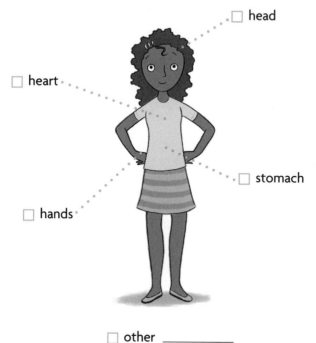

☐ head

☐ heart

☐ stomach

☐ hands

☐ other _____

# Alone or Lonely?

Being alone doesn't always make you feel lonely. Take this quiz to see how you tend to react to being by yourself. Pick the answer that is most like how you would respond.

**1.** All my friends sign up for the soccer team, but I'm not really that interested. I decide to

   **a.** sign up anyway, so I'm not left out.

   **b.** do my own thing and figure I'll get together with my friends at other times.

**2.** My parents are taking me to dinner with my father's boss, who has no kids my age. Before we go, I

   **a.** complain that it will be boring and I won't know a soul.

   **b.** decide that I might enjoy talking to someone new. When I'm there, I'll look for a chance to ask questions.

**3.** It's Friday and I'm ready for fun! But everyone I call has plans for the weekend. I react by

   **a.** pacing the floor, sure that I'll never see my friends again.

   **b.** digging out one of my favorite hobbies or curling up in front of a movie I love.

**4.** I'm at my uncle's wedding, but my entire dance troupe is at a competition I wanted to attend. At the wedding reception, I

a. pout all evening, thinking about what I'm missing.

b. look for other kids my age that I can have fun with. I can even do some dancing right here!

# Answers

If you had mostly **a** answers, you enjoy your friends. Great! Just be careful not to depend on them too much for your entertainment and fun. If you keep wishing that you were somewhere else, you'll feel lonelier than you need to feel. Focus on enjoying the here and now, and the time will move along faster. No matter how much fun you think others are having, a little time apart may make all of you appreciate your times together more.

If you had mostly **b** answers, you may prefer to be somewhere else, with people you know and enjoy, but you have a knack for making the best of any situation. Good for you! Being flexible is an important skill to learn. By focusing on the people and activities at your fingertips, you will help everyone have more fun. And guess what? Your independent thinking may be one of the things your friends admire most about you.

# Mood Minder: I'm Lonely

Loneliness can make you sad if you focus on what you aren't able to do. Distracting yourself can get your mind off feeling lonely.

What activities could I do the next time I feel lonely?

_____

_____

Sometimes you may feel lonely because you're focusing too much on trying to be with just one or two people.

I do have other friends I haven't seen in a while, such as

_____

_____

It's easy to stay focused on one activity—or one set of friends—but remember that finding new friends might relieve your loneliness.

What new activity or club could I try to meet more people?

_____

_____

If you think too much about someone you miss, you might become a drag on the people you're with now. Stay in the moment. Suggest a fun activity to the people you're with, and you'll have more fun—and feel better, too.

Some fun things I could suggest to the people I'm with right now:

☐ Playing a game

☐ Watching a movie

☐ Going for ice cream

☐ Taking a walk

☐ Singing together

☐ Baking or cooking

☐ Listening (or dancing) to music

☐ Other _____
_____
_____

# Feeling Sad

Sadness is a part of everyone's life. When you are sad, you may cry, become quiet, or act grumpy around others. At times, it can seem tough to do even the simplest things. Think of a time when you felt sad.

I felt sad when _____

_____

_____

My body reacted to my sadness. I felt this emotion most in my

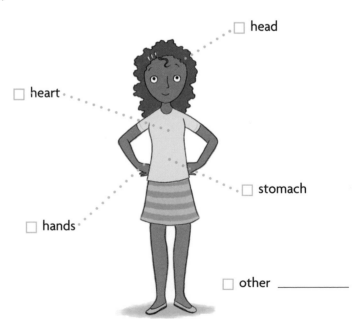

☐ head

☐ heart

☐ stomach

☐ hands

☐ other _____

Some people could tell I was sad because I _____

_____

_____

_____

_____

_____

_____

Something that helped was _____

_____

_____

_____

_____

_____

_____

_____

# Mood Minder: I'm Sad

Feeling sad can interfere with friendships, family life, school-work, and activities. One of the best things you can do is tell someone how you feel.

Two people I can talk to are

_____ and _____

Using your artistic talents may help you express your feelings. Which of these art activities would you do when you're feeling down? I would

☐ draw.                ☐ dance.              ☐ sculpt.

☐ paint.               ☐ sing.               ☐ other _____

☐ write poetry.        ☐ keep a journal.     _____

When you are sad, it can seem hard to drag yourself through the day. But getting up and going is always your best defense. How do you like to get your body moving? I like to

☐ walk outside.        ☐ run.                ☐ dance.

☐ bicycle.             ☐ exercise            ☐ play sports.
                         indoors.
                                              ☐ other _____
                       ☐ swim.
                                              _____

You experience life with all five senses. When you feel sad, changing some of the things you see, hear, feel, smell, or taste may help. The next time you're blue, try some of these sensory experiences.

## Sight
- Watch an uplifting movie.
- Read an inspiring book.
- Open the curtains and let in the light.

## Sound
- Put on some soothing music.
- Call to hear a friend's voice.
- Listen to the birds sing.

## Smell
- Breathe in fresh air.
- Smell a flower.
- Notice the aromas of favorite foods cooking.

## Touch
- Ask for a hug.
- Have your shoulders rubbed.
- Take a warm bubble bath.

## Taste
- Drink some hot tea.
- Share lunch with someone who cares about you.

Sometimes sadness runs deep. If you experience any of the feelings below, show this page to your parents and talk about whether a professional could help you. It may not mean you're depressed, but your sadness may need extra care. Do you

☐ have sadness that lasts more than two weeks?

☐ feel tired all the time?

☐ have difficulty concentrating?

☐ often feel angry or irritable?

☐ not feel like doing things you usually enjoy?

☐ have frequent stomach-aches or headaches?

☐ have bad feelings about yourself?

☐ think a lot about death or suicide?*

☐ feel you could hurt your-self or someone else?*

*Note: Even if you didn't check other items, if you checked either of the last two, tell an adult right away and ask to talk to a psychologist or medical doctor.

# Feeling Grief

Grief is the mixture of painful emotions you may experience when you lose someone or something you care about. When someone you love dies, you lose a pet, or a good friend moves away, it can feel as though your whole heart aches. The good news is you can let yourself be sad, learn from it, and get through it.

I felt grief when _____

_____

_____

_____

_____

_____

_____

_____

_____

My body reacted to my grief. I felt this emotion most in my

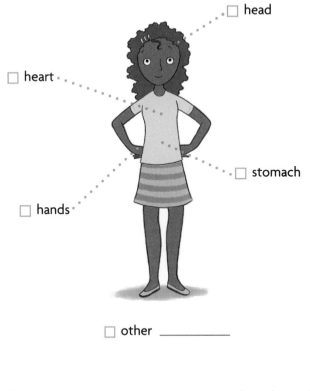

☐ head

☐ heart

☐ stomach

☐ hands

☐ other _____

I talked to _____ about how I felt.

It helped me a little bit when someone said, " _____

_____

_____

_____

_____."

# Mood Minder: I'm Grieving

You may experience many feelings as you adjust to your loss. No matter how much it hurts, one of the best things you can do is to talk to someone who understands.

Someone I can talk to about my grief is _____

_____

Keep the person or pet you are grieving for in your heart. Remember something nice that happened with him or her.

One special memory I have is _____

_____

_____

_____

Keeping a special reminder of the person or pet you are missing may help you. Put it on display or keep it someplace where only you will see it.

A special reminder that I have is

_____

_____

_____

Memories can be comforting and pleasant. But dwelling nonstop on sad thoughts will only make you sadder. Remember to direct most of your energy to what you are doing right now, and look forward to good things in the future.

One thing I am looking forward to is _____

_____

_____

_____

_____

_____

_____

# Big, Bad Circles

When you're upset, your feelings and actions can go around and around and make you feel worse. Do you recognize these nasty circles of thought?

You **feel** angry because a friend went to the game without you.

**Anger Circle**

You **think** she doesn't like you anymore.

You **act** rudely when you see her again and stomp away.

Your friend **reacts** by saying you acted rudely.

You **feel** nervous about giving a school speech.

You **think** you are going to mess up.

You **act** jumpy and can't concentrate.

You **react** by making mistakes you wouldn't have made if you had been calm.

**Anxiety Circle**

**Learn to break the circle!**

Can you think of a negative circle you've been in lately?

Here's how I felt:

      ☐ Sad           ☐ Anxious

      ☐ Angry      ☐ Other _____

Feeling this way made me think negatively. One thing

I thought was _____

_____

Thinking negatively made me act _____

Here's what I did: _____

_____

Someone reacted to me by _____

_____

_____

This made me

☐ feel the same way I felt to start with, or worse!

☐ think that those negative thoughts about myself
    were right.

☐ act even more negatively than I did in the beginning.

# Positive Circles

The best way to stop a negative circle is to replace it with a positive circle. Start by changing how you think and act. Eventually this will change how you feel, too. For every negative thought you have about yourself, think about why it might not be true.

Here are some practice thoughts to work on:

**If I think,** "I'm going to fail this test," **I could stop and tell myself,** "That's probably not true. I can prepare by

_____

_____."

**If I think,** "I'm not likable," **I could stop and tell myself,** "That's probably not true. Not everyone may like me, but my friends like me because

_____

_____."

**If I think,** "Nobody wants to spend time with me," **I could stop and tell myself,** "That's probably not true. I could call these people:

_____."

With a little practice, you can create positive circles wherever you are. Try it!

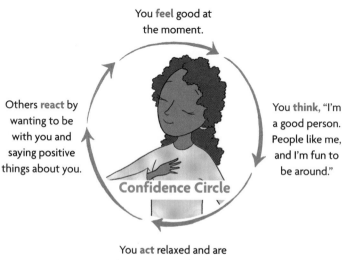

You **feel** good at the moment.

Others **react** by wanting to be with you and saying positive things about you.

You **think**, "I'm a good person. People like me, and I'm fun to be around."

**Confidence Circle**

You **act** relaxed and are pleasant to people. You are interested in others.

And the circle keeps going around—this time in a good direction!

# Congratulations!

Using your journal, you've learned many ways to feel better when you are upset. Look through the list below and mark some of your favorite strategies:

When I'm upset, I can

☐ tell myself this positive thing: _____

_____

_____

_____

_____

☐ talk to _____

or _____

☐ get moving—walk, play a sport, or dance.

☐ express myself creatively through writing, music, or another art form.

☐ change my surroundings.

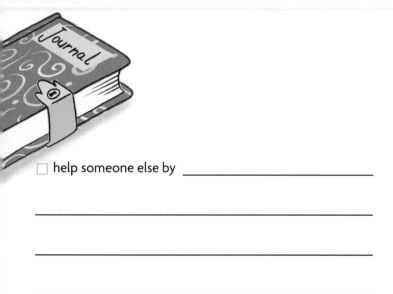

☐ help someone else by _____

_____

_____

_____

☐ take care of myself—eat healthily,
get enough sleep, and have fun.

☐ relax!

# A Letter to Myself

Remember, you are the only **you** there is. You have unique strengths. If you like who you are, others will like you, too. Be nice to yourself! Imagine that you are your own best friend, and write yourself a letter. Give it a read whenever you need a boost.

Dear _____,
(your name)

Even though you feel down sometimes, here are some positive words that describe you—and I'm checking all that apply:

☐ Happy

☐ Funny

☐ Kind

☐ Caring

☐ Sweet

☐ Sensitive

☐ Creative

☐ Clever

☐ Smart

☐ Organized

☐ Coordinated

☐ Studious

☐ Level-headed

☐ Calm

☐ Attractive

☐ Nice hair

☐ Pretty eyes

☐ Good reader

☐ Talented

☐ Brave

☐ A leader

☐ Hardworking

☐ Good speaker

☐ Good writer

☐ Musical

☐ Generous

I know other good things about you, too. For instance,

_____

_____

Other people like you, too. Someone once said this

nice thing about you: " _____

_____

_____ ."

You are also a thoughtful person. For example, it was

really nice when you _____

_____

_____

You're a good person and a good friend!

Love, _____

# Journal Pages

Now you know a lot about
managing your emotions. Don't stop paying
attention to how you feel. Keep sharing
what you think, and remember to use your
Mood Minders. Use the rest of your journal
to record what happens during your days.
Have fun!

# My Journal Entry

Date _____

Today a

☐ crazy      ☐ great      ☐ irritating

☐ funny      ☐ sad      ☐ goofy

☐ embarrassing      ☐ scary      ☐ happy

thing happened. It went like this: _____

_____

_____

_____

_____

On the happiness scale, today was

☐ soaring.      ☐ good.      ☐ just so-so.      ☐ the pits.

I'll tell you why: _____

_____

_____

_____

_____

_____

Here's something I could do about the way I feel: _____

_____

_____

_____

Other thoughts about the day: _____

_____

_____

_____

_____

_____

_____

_____

_____

_____

_____

_____

_____

# My Journal Entry

Date _____

Today a

☐ crazy        ☐ great        ☐ irritating

☐ funny        ☐ sad        ☐ goofy

☐ embarrassing        ☐ scary        ☐ happy

thing happened. It went like this: _____

_____

_____

_____

_____

On the happiness scale, today was

☐ soaring.      ☐ good.      ☐ just so-so.      ☐ the pits.

I'll tell you why: _____

_____

_____

_____

_____

_____

Here's something I could do about the way I feel: _____

_____

_____

_____

Other thoughts about the day: _____

_____

_____

_____

_____

_____

_____

_____

_____

_____

_____

# My Journal Entry

Date _____

Today a

☐ crazy       ☐ great       ☐ irritating

☐ funny       ☐ sad       ☐ goofy

☐ embarrassing       ☐ scary       ☐ happy

thing happened. It went like this: _____

_____

_____

_____

_____

On the happiness scale, today was

☐ soaring.    ☐ good.    ☐ just so-so.    ☐ the pits.

I'll tell you why: _____

_____

_____

_____

_____

_____

Here's something I could do about the way I feel: _____

_____

_____

_____

Other thoughts about the day: _____

_____

_____

_____

_____

_____

_____

_____

_____

_____

_____

# My Journal Entry

Date _____

Today a

☐ crazy       ☐ great       ☐ irritating

☐ funny       ☐ sad       ☐ goofy

☐ embarrassing       ☐ scary       ☐ happy

thing happened. It went like this: _____

_____

_____

_____

_____

On the happiness scale, today was

☐ soaring.       ☐ good.       ☐ just so-so.       ☐ the pits.

I'll tell you why: _____

_____

_____

_____

_____

_____

Here's something I could do about the way I feel: _____

_____

_____

_____

Other thoughts about the day: _____

_____

_____

_____

_____

_____

_____

_____

_____

_____

_____

_____

_____

# My Journal Entry

Date _____

Today a

☐ crazy        ☐ great        ☐ irritating

☐ funny        ☐ sad          ☐ goofy

☐ embarrassing ☐ scary        ☐ happy

thing happened. It went like this: _____

_____

_____

_____

_____

On the happiness scale, today was

☐ soaring.    ☐ good.    ☐ just so-so.    ☐ the pits.

I'll tell you why: _____

_____

_____

_____

_____

_____

Here's something I could do about the way I feel: _____

_____

_____

_____

Other thoughts about the day: _____

_____

_____

_____

_____

_____

_____

_____

_____

_____

_____

_____

# My Journal Entry

Date _____

Today a

☐ crazy ☐ great ☐ irritating

☐ funny ☐ sad ☐ goofy

☐ embarrassing ☐ scary ☐ happy

thing happened. It went like this: _____

_____

_____

_____

_____

On the happiness scale, today was

☐ soaring. ☐ good. ☐ just so-so. ☐ the pits.

I'll tell you why: _____

_____

_____

_____

_____

Here's something I could do about the way I feel: _____

_____

_____

_____

Other thoughts about the day: _____

_____

_____

_____

_____

_____

_____

_____

_____

_____

_____

_____

# My Journal Entry

Date _____

Today a

☐ crazy        ☐ great        ☐ irritating

☐ funny        ☐ sad          ☐ goofy

☐ embarrassing ☐ scary        ☐ happy

thing happened. It went like this: _____

_____

_____

_____

_____

On the happiness scale, today was

☐ soaring.     ☐ good.      ☐ just so-so.     ☐ the pits.

I'll tell you why: _____

_____

_____

_____

_____

_____

Here's something I could do about the way I feel: _____

_____

_____

_____

Other thoughts about the day: _____

_____

_____

_____

_____

_____

_____

_____

_____

_____

_____

_____

All done?
You can make extra journal pages
in any notebook you have.
Keep on writing!

# Write to us!

At American Girl, we love hearing from girls just like you. Tell us what you think of *The Feelings Book Journal*! Send us your questions and ideas.

Write to us at:
Feelings Book Editor
American Girl
8400 Fairway Place
Middleton, WI 53562

# Here are some other
# American Girl books you might like:

American Girl offers a family of body and mind books
for girls just like you to turn to for advice about growing up.
Millions of younger girls have used *The Care & Keeping of
You 1* to get started, as well as its companion, *The
Care & Keeping of You 1 Journal. The Feelings Book* along
with this companion journal help you handle the new
emotions you may be feeling. And when you're ready,
*The Care & Keeping of You 2: The Body Book for Older Girls*
will help guide you through the physical, emotional, and
social changes that you may need help understanding.

Each sold separately. Find more books online at americangirl.com.